T0083137

Move him into the sun

Bob Chilcott

for upper voices, SATB, and piano (with snare drum, tenor drum, and solo cello) or chamber orchestra

Vocal score

MUSIC DEPARTMENT

OXFORD
UNIVERSITY PRESS

OXFORD
UNIVERSITY PRESS

Great Clarendon Street, Oxford OX2 6DP,
United Kingdom

Oxford University Press is a department of the University of Oxford.
It furthers the University's objective of excellence in research, scholarship,
and education by publishing worldwide. Oxford is a registered trade mark of
Oxford University Press in the UK and in certain other countries

© Oxford University Press 2018

Bob Chilcott has asserted his right under the Copyright, Designs
and Patents Act, 1988, to be identified as the Composer of this Work

First published 2018

Impression: 1

All rights reserved. No part of this publication may be reproduced,
stored in a retrieval system, or transmitted, in any form or by any means,
without the prior permission in writing of Oxford University Press

Permission to perform this work in public (except in the course of divine worship)
should normally be obtained from a local performing right licensing organization,
unless the owner or the occupier of the premises being used already holds
a licence from such an organization. Likewise, permission to make and
exploit a recording of these works should be obtained from a
local mechanical copyright licensing organization

Enquiries concerning reproduction outside the scope of the above
should be directed to the Music Rights Department, Oxford University Press,
at music.permissions.uk@oup.com or at the address above

ISBN 978–0–19–341082–4

Music origination by Katie Johnston
Printed in Great Britain on acid-free paper by
Halstan & Co. Ltd, Amersham, Bucks.

Contents

Texts	iv
1. Song of Songs	8
2. Spring Offensive	20
3. Apologia pro Poemate Meo	33
4. Futility	38
5. Winter Song	51
Snare Drum part	62
Tenor Drum part	63
Solo Cello part	64

Composer's note

Wilfred Owen is known to many as the poet who died a young man, and who wrote so vividly and emotionally about the horror and futility of war. However, other passionate themes are ever-present in his poetry, the two principal ones perhaps being those of beauty and love, the latter not only for the natural world around him but also for his fellow human beings, comrades, and friends. In this piece the image of the sun, as a source of light, life, and energy, is the one that I have focused on. Portrayed here largely by the upper-voice choir, it ultimately becomes a source of redemption and an expression of feeling at one with life, articulated so beautifully in Owen's poetry.

Commissioned by the Trustees of the St Chad's Music Festival and Shrewsbury Bookfest in memory of Wilfred Owen, the Shropshire soldier-poet who was born in Oswestry on 18 March 1893, lived in Shrewsbury from 1907, and was killed in action near Ors in Northern France on 4 November 1918.

Duration: *c.*25 minutes

An accompaniment for small orchestra (2fl, ob, cl, bsn, hn in F, timp, perc (2 players), pno, str) is available on hire/rental from the publisher or appropriate agent. For orchestral performances, the piano part available on hire/rental should be used, rather than the part in the vocal score. The parts for percussion in movement two and solo cello in movement three are identical in the vocal score and orchestral set.

Texts

1. Song of Songs

Extract from 'The Promisers' (Upper voices)

When I awoke, the glancing day looked gay;
The air said: Fare you fleetly; you will meet him!
And when the prosp'rous sun was well begun
I heard a bird say: Sweetly you shall greet him!

'Song of Songs' (SATB)

Sing me at morn but only with your laugh;
Even as Spring that laugheth into leaf;
Even as Love that laugheth after Life.

Sing me but only with your speech all day,
As voluble leaflets do; let viols die;
The least word of your lips is melody!

Sing me at eve but only with your sigh!
Like lifting seas it solaceth; breathe so,
Slowly and low, the sense that no songs say.

Sing me at midnight with your murmurous heart!
Let youth's immortal-moaning chords be heard
Throbbing through you, and sobbing, unsubdued.

2. Spring Offensive

Extract from 'The Promisers' (Upper voices)

The sun felt strong and bold upon my shoulder;
It hung, it clung as it were my friend's arm.
The birds fifed on before, shrill-piping pipers,
Right down to town; and there they ceased to charm.

Extract from 'Spring Offensive' (SATB)

Hour after hour they ponder the warm field
And the far valley behind, where the buttercups
Had blessed with gold their slow boots coming up;
When even the little brambles would not yield,
But clutched and clung to them like sorrowing arms;
They breathe like trees unstirred.

Till like a cold gust thrills the little word
At which each body and its soul begird†
And tighten them for battle. No alarms
Of bugles, no high flags, no clamorous haste—
Only a lift and flare of eyes that faced
The sun, like a friend with whom their love is done.
O larger shone that smile against the sun—
Mightier than his whose bounty these have spurned.

† embrace; encompass

3. Apologia pro Poemate Meo

Extract from 'Apologia pro Poemate Meo'

I, too, saw God through mud—
The mud that cracked on cheeks when wretches smiled.
War brought more glory to their eyes than blood,
And gave their laughs more glee than shakes a child.

I, too, have dropped off Fear—
Behind the barrage, dead as my platoon,
And sailed my spirit surging light and clear
Past the entanglement where hopes lay strewn.

I have made fellowships—
Untold of happy lovers in old song.
For love is not the binding of fair lips
With the soft silk of eyes that look and long.

I have perceived much beauty
In the hoarse oaths that kept our courage straight;
Heard music in the silentness of duty;
Found peace where shell-storms spouted reddest spate.

4. Futility

Extract from 'Sonnet, To a child' (Upper voices)

To all men else uncouth;
Save me, who know your smile comes very old,
Learnt of the happy dead that laughed with gods;
For earlier suns than ours have lent you gold;
Sly fauns and trees have given you jigs and nods.

'Futility' (SATB)

Move him into the sun—
Gently its touch awoke him once,
At home, whispering of fields half-sown.
Always it woke him, even in France,
Until this morning and this snow.
If anything might rouse him now
The kind old sun will know.

Think how it wakes the seeds—
Woke, once, the clays of a cold star.
Are limbs, so dear achieved, are sides
Full-nerved—still warm—too hard to stir?
Was it for this the clay grew tall?
—O what made fatuous sunbeams toil
To break earth's sleep at all?

5. Winter Song

Extract from 'Winter Song'

From off your face, into the winds of winter,
The sun-brown and the summer-gold are blowing;
But they shall gleam again with spiritual glinter,
When paler beauty on your brows falls snowing,
And through those snows my looks shall be soft-going.

Extract from 'Happiness'

The sun may cleanse,
And time, and starlight. Life will sing sweet songs,
And gods will show us pleasure more than men's.

Texts from *Wilfred Owen: The War Poems*, ed. Jon Stallworthy (1935–2014) (Chatto & Windus, 1994).

Move him into the sun

Commissioned by the Trustees of the St Chad's Music Festival and Shrewsbury Bookfest in memory of Wilfred Owen

Move him into the sun

1. Song of Songs

Wilfred Owen (1893–1918)

BOB CHILCOTT

© Oxford University Press 2018. Text from 'Wilfred Owen: The War Poems', ed. Jon Stallworthy (1935–2014) (Chatto & Windus, 1994).

Printed in Great Britain

OXFORD UNIVERSITY PRESS, MUSIC DEPARTMENT, GREAT CLARENDON STREET, OXFORD OX2 6DP

The Moral Rights of the Composer have been asserted. Photocopying this copyright material is ILLEGAL.

7
meet him! And when the prosp'- rous sun was
10
well be - gun I heard a bird say: Sweet-ly you shall
3
13
greet him!

16
S.
A.
f
ff
Sing me at morn but on - ly with your laugh;
T.
B.
f
ff
ff
18
f
ff
E - ven as Spring that laugh - eth in - to leaf;
f
ff
f
ff
20
mf
E - ven as Love that laugh - eth af - ter Life.
mf
mf

22
f
mf
Sing me, sing me, sing me,
Sing me, sing, sing me, sing
Sing, sing me, sing, sing me,
Sing, sing me, sing me,
25
sing me, sing me.
me, sing me, sing me.
sing me, sing me.
sing me, sing me.

28
mp
(mp)
Sing me but on - ly with your speech all day,
mp
mp
mp
mp
32
mf
As vo - lu - ble leaf - lets do; let vi - ols die; The least word of your lips is
mf
Let vi - ols die; The least word of your lips is
mf
Vi - ols die; The least word
mf
The least word
mf

35
me - lo - dy, me - lo - dy,
me - lo - dy, of your lips is me - lo -
of your lips is me - lo - dy, me - lo -
of your lips is me - lo -

37
p
me - lo - dy!
p
- dy!
p
- dy!
p
- dy!
p

41
UPPER VOICES
p
Sing me, sing me,
BASSES
p
B.
Sing me at eve but on - ly with your sigh! Like

44
UPPER VOICES
sing me, sing me. Sing
Breathe so,
p
S. A.
Breathe, breathe
Breathe so,
p
T. B.
lift - ing seas it sol - ac - eth; breathe, breathe

47
me, sing me,
Slow - ly and low, the
so, Slow - ly and low, the
Slow - ly and low, the
so, Slow - ly and low,
50
sing me, sing
sense that no songs say.
mp
sense that no songs, no songs
sense that no songs, no songs
mp
the sense that no songs say.
mp

53
me, sing me.
say. Sing me, sing
say. Sing, sing me,
Sing me.
56
S. A.
p
me.
T. B.
p
p
60
p mp
murm - 'rous heart!
Sing me at mid - night with your murm - 'rous, murm - 'rous
p mp
mp

64
mf
heart! Let youth's chords be
mf
heart! Let youth's im - mor - tal - moan - ing chords be
mf
67
mp
heard Throb - bing through you, and
mp
mp
70
sob - bing, un - sub - dued.

73
S.
A.
T.
B.
cresc.
Sing we, sing we,
Sing we, sing, sing
Sing we, sing, sing
76
mf cresc.
Sing, sing we, sing we,
sing we, sing we, sing
we, sing we, sing, we, sing,
we, sing we, sing,

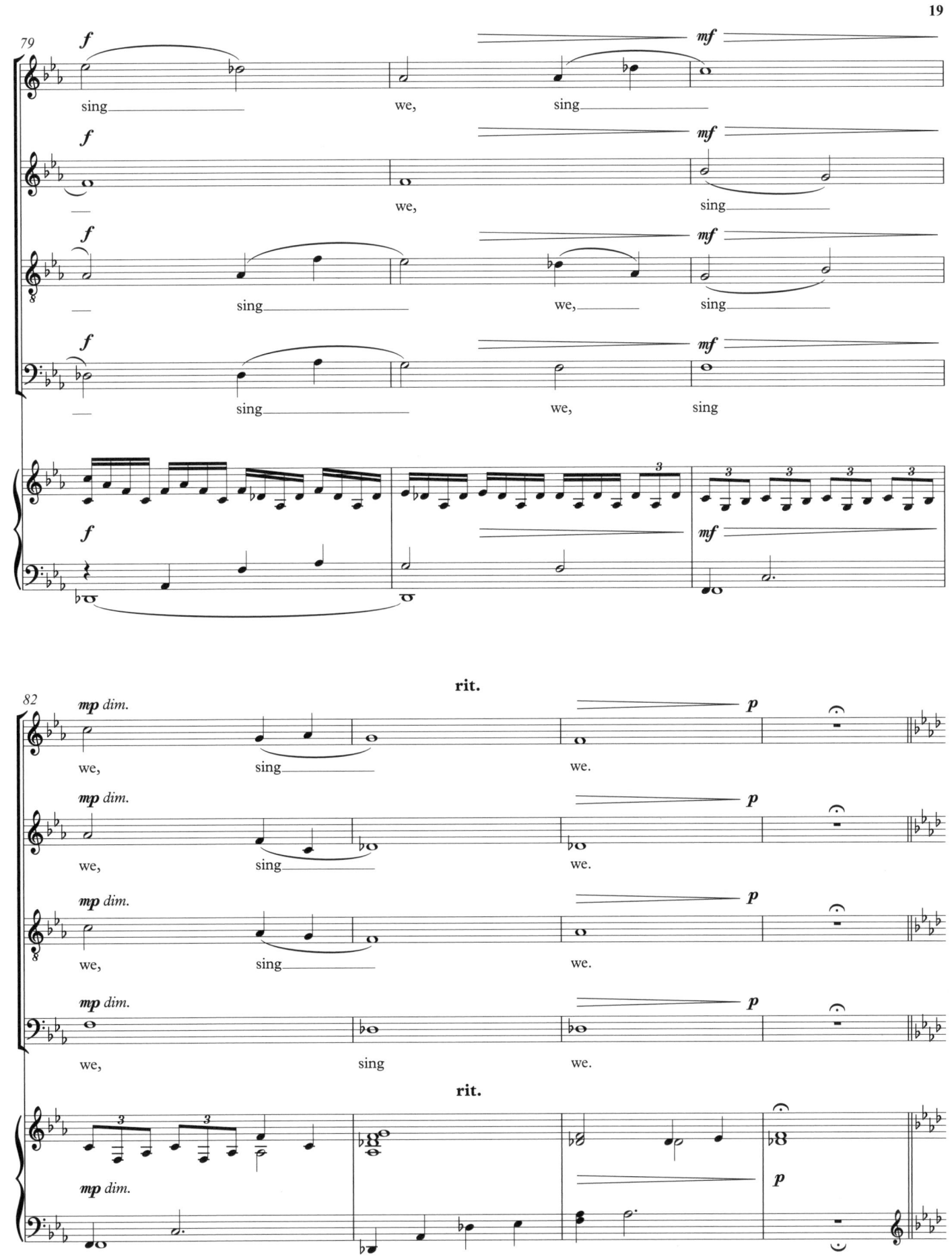
79
f
mf
sing we, sing
f
mf
we, sing
f
mf
sing we, sing
f
mf
sing we, sing
f
mf
rit.
82
mp dim.
p
we, sing we.
mp dim.
p
we, sing we.
mp dim.
p
we, sing we.
mp dim.
p
we, sing we.
rit.
mp dim.
p

2. Spring Offensive

7
birds fifed on be - fore, shrill - pi - ping pi - pers, Right down to town; and there they ceased to
10
charm. Right down to town; and there they ceased to charm. The sun felt
13
strong, the sun felt strong, the sun felt

17
SNARE DRUM
TENOR DRUM
mp
UPPER VOICES
strong.
mp
21
SNARE DRUM
TENOR DRUM
Hour af-ter hour,
mp
Hour af-ter hour,
unis. mf
the sun felt
S.
Hour af-ter hour
they pon - der the warm field
mf
A.
Hour af-ter hour
they pon - der the warm field,
T. B.
Hour af-ter hour they pon - der the warm field,
mf

24
The val-ley be - hind,
mp
strong.
The val-ley be - hind,
mp
And the far val-ley be - hind,
the val - ley be -
mp
the val-ley be - hind,
the val - ley be -
mp
the val-ley be-hind, the val - ley be -

27
mf
mf
unis. mf
the sun felt strong.
mp
Had
mf
hind,
mp
3
3
where the but-ter - cups Had blessed, with
mf
- hind,
mp
3
3
where the but-ter - cups Had blessed, had
mf
- hind,
mp
Had blessed, had
mf
mp

30
UPPER VOICES
blessed with gold their slow, slow
mf
S.
gold their slow boots com - ing up,
mf
A.
blessed with gold, with gold, their slow, their slow boots
mf
T.
B.
blessed with gold, with gold, their slow, their slow boots
mf
33
f
boots com - ing up, com - ing
f
com - ing up; When e - ven the lit - tle bram - bles would not
f
com - ing up; When e - ven the lit - tle bram - bles would not
f
com - ing up; When e - ven the lit - tle bram - bles would not
f

36
mf
up.
mf
yield, not yield.
mf
yield, not yield.
mf
yield, not yield.
mp
But clutched and clung to them like
mf
mp
39
(BASSES)
B.
3
sor - row - ing arms; They breathe like trees un - stirred.

† embrace; encompass

51
SNARE DRUM
TENOR DRUM
mp
S.
A.
no high flags, no clam - 'rous haste, On - ly a
T.
no high flags, no clam - 'rous haste, On - ly a
B.
no high flag, no clam - 'rous haste, On - ly a
54
SNARE DRUM
TENOR DRUM
mf cresc.
S.
lift and flare of eyes that faced The sun, like a friend, a friend with
A.
lift and flare of eyes that faced The sun, a friend with
T.
lift and flare of eyes that faced The sun, a friend with
B.
lift of eyes that faced The sun, a friend with

57
SNARE DRUM
TENOR DRUM
f
mf
UPPER VOICES
O larg - er, larg - er
S.
whom their love is done. O larg - er shone that
A.
whom their love is done. O larg - er
T.
whom their love is done, is done. O larg - er
B.
whom their love is done. O larg - er
3

60
ff
shone that smile, that smile a - gainst the
smile a - gainst the sun, Might - ier than his whose boun - ty these have
shone that smile a - gainst The sun, than his whose boun - ty these have
shone that smile a - gainst The sun, than his whose boun - ty these have
shone that smile a - gainst The sun, than his whose boun - ty these have

63
f
mf
f
mf
sun.
spurned, have spurned.
mf
spurned, have spurned, spurned.
mf
spurned, have spurned, have spurned.
spurned, have spurned.
mf

67
TENOR DRUM
mp
UPPER VOICES
p
The
mp
p
72
UPPER VOICES
sun felt strong and bold u - pon my shoul - der, the sun felt
rit.
Slow
75
strong.
pp

3. *Apologia pro Poemate Meo*

12
poco rit.
gave their laughs more glee than shakes a child, a child.
mp
16
a tempo
SOLO CELLO
p espress.
p espress.
I, too, have dropped off Fear,
Be - hind the bar - rage, dead as my pla -
a tempo
p
20
mf
mf
-toon,
And sailed my spi - rit surg-ing light and clear
mf

24
mp
mp
Past the en - tan - gle-ment where hopes lay strewn, lay strewn.
mp
28
mf
mf
I have made fel - low- ships, Un - told of hap - py lov - ers in old
mf
31
song. For love is not the bind - ing of fair lips

34
p
p
mf
With the soft silk of eyes that look and long.
I
p
38
mf
have per-ceived much beau - ty
In the hoarse oaths that kept our cour - age
mf
41
mp
mp
straight;
Heard mu - sic in the si - lent - ness of
mp

44
p
p
du - ty;
Found peace where shell - storms
p
47
spout - ed red - dest spate,
found peace,
found
rit.
52
pp
pp
peace,
found
peace.
rit.
pp

4. Futility

With stillness ♩ = c.46
UPPER VOICES
p
To all men, Save me, who know your smile comes
S. A.
T. B.
With stillness ♩ = c.46
p sost.
con Ped.
7
UPPER VOICES
ve - ry old, Learnt of the hap - py dead that laughed with gods; For
13
ear - lier suns than ours have lent you gold; Sly fauns and trees have giv'n you jigs and

19
nods.
Save me, save me, save
25
me.
30
UPPER VOICES
Save me, save me.
S. A.
p
mp
Move him, move him in - to the sun, the
T. B.
p
mp
mp

35
S.
A.
sun, Gent - ly its touch,
sun, Gent - ly its touch, gent - ly its touch a -
T.
B.
sun, Gent - ly its touch,
40
UPPER VOICES
mp
p
Save me, save me.
S.
A.
p
- woke him once, At home, whis - per-ing of
T.
B.
p
p
fields half - sown. Al - ways it woke him,
45
mp
S.
A.
fields half - sown. Al - ways it woke him, e - ven in
mp
T.
B.
fields half - sown. Al - ways it woke him,
mp

50
UPPER VOICES
mp
p
Save me, save me.
S. A.
p
France, Un - til this morn-ing and this snow.
T. B.
p
p
55
S.
mp
mf
If a - ny-thing might rouse him now The
A.
mp
mf
If a - ny-thing might rouse him now The
T.
mp
mf
If a - ny-thing might rouse him now The
B.
mp
mf
If a - ny-thing might rouse him now The
mp
mf

60
kind old sun will know, the kind old sun will know. Move him
kind sun will know, the kind sun will know. Move him
kind old sun will know, the kind old sun will know. Move him
sun will know, the sun will know. Move
65
in - to the sun.
in - to the sun.
in - to the sun.
him in - to the sun.
70

75
mf
Woke, once, the
mf
Woke, once, the
mf
Woke, once, the
p
3
mp
mf
Think how it wakes the seeds.
Woke, once, the
mp
mf
80
clays, the clays of a cold star.
p
clays, the clays of a cold, cold star.
p
clays, the clays of a cold, cold star.
p
clays, the clays of a cold, cold star.
p

85
p
mp
mf
Think how it wakes the seeds. Woke, once, the
Think how it wakes the seeds. Woke, once, the
Woke, once, the
Woke, once, the
90
UPPER VOICES
Save, save me. Are
S.
clays, the clays of a cold star. Are limbs, are
A.
clays, the clays of a cold star. Are limbs, are
T.
clays, the clays of a cold star. Are limbs, are
B.
clays, of a cold star. Are limbs, are
f

95
limbs so dear a - chieved, are sides Full -
limbs, so dear a - chieved, are sides Full -
limbs, so dear a - chieved, are sides Full -
limbs, so dear a - chieved, are sides Full -
limbs, so dear a - chieved, are sides Full -
99
-nerved, still warm?
mf
-nerved, still warm, too hard to stir?
mf
-nerved, still warm, too hard to stir?
mf
-nerved still warm, too hard to stir?
mf
-nerved, still warm, too hard to stir?
mf

104
mf
p
Save me, save me.
p
108
pp
p
113
p
mp
p
T.
Was it for this the clay grew tall, grew
p
mp
p
B.
Was it for this the clay grew tall, grew
mp
p

118
UPPER VOICES
p dolce
Save me, save me,
S.
p dolce
O what made fat - uous
A.
p dolce
O what made fat - uous
T.
p dolce
tall? O what made fat - uous
B.
p dolce
tall? O what made fat - uous
123
mf
save me, save me. O
sun - beams toil To break earth's sleep, at all?
sun - beams toil To break earth's sleep, earth's sleep
sun - beams toil To break earth's sleep, earth's sleep
sun - beams toil To break earth's sleep, earth's sleep

128
f
mf dim.
what, O what made fat - uous sun - beams toil To
mf
f
mf dim.
O what made fat - uous sun - beams toil To
mf
f
mf dim.
at all? What made sun - - beams toil To
mf
f
mf dim.
at all? What made sun - - beams toil To
mf
f
mf dim.
at all? What made sun - beams toil To
mf
f
mf dim.
133
p
break earth's sleep at all?
p
break earth's sleep, to break
p
break earth's sleep, to break, to
p
break earth's sleep, sleep, to break, to
p
break earth's sleep, to break, to

138
Save me, save me.
earth's sleep at all?
break earth's sleep at all?
break earth's sleep at all?
break sleep at all?
p
143
UPPER VOICES
p
Save me, save
148
UPPER VOICES
me.
mp
p
S. A.
Move him, move him in - to the sun, the sun,
T. B.
p
mp
mp

153
mp
p
Save me, save me,
p
move him, move him, move him
p
p
160
rit.
save me, save me.
in - to the sun.
rit.
pp

5. Winter Song

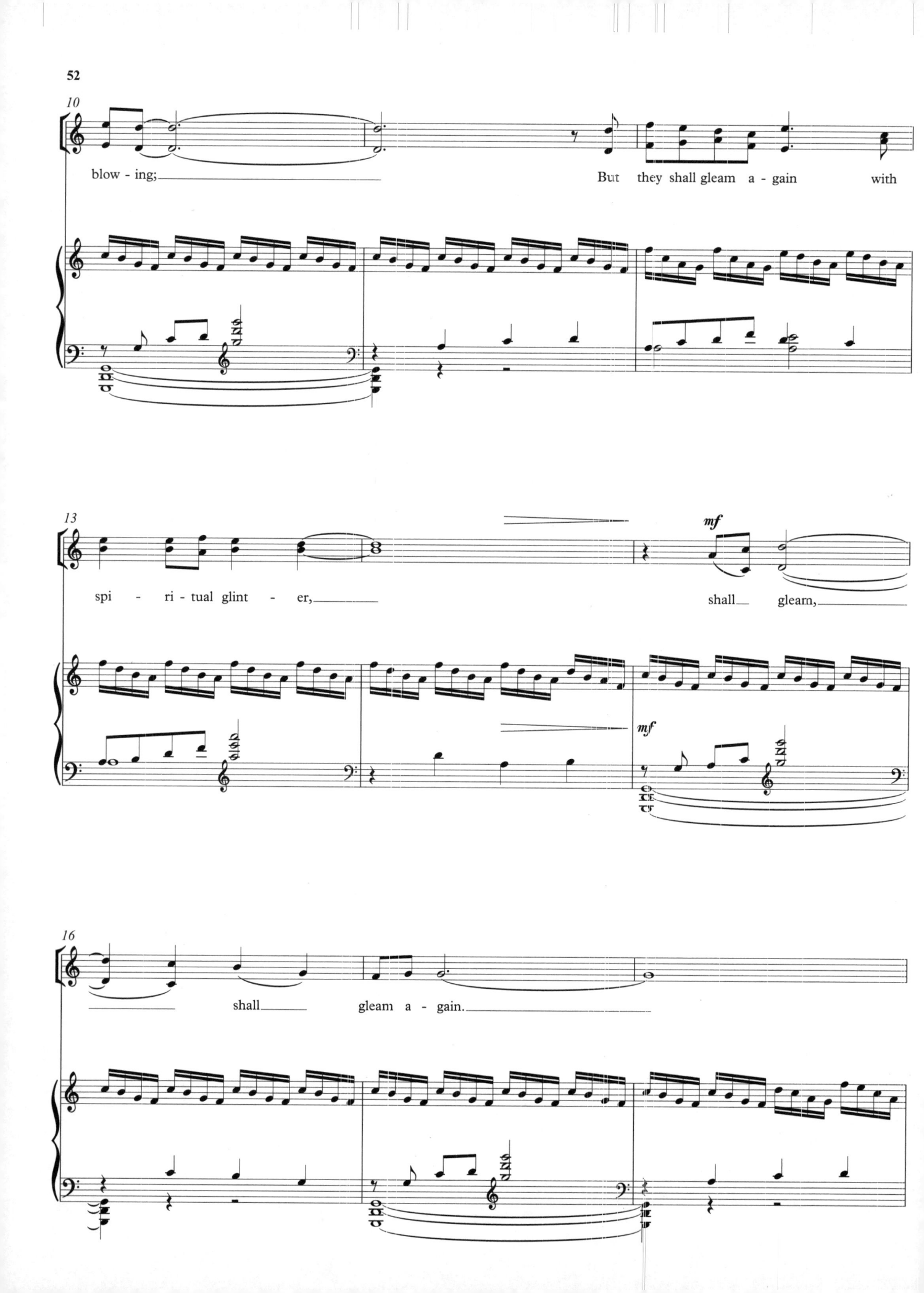
10
blow - ing;
But they shall gleam a - gain with
13
spi - ri - tual glint - er,
mf
shall gleam,
mf
16
shall gleam a - gain.

From off your face, in - to the winds of win - ter,
19
f
ff
From off your face, your face, in - to the winds of win - ter, of
f
ff
ff
22
f
ff
are
win - ter, The sun - brown and the sum - mer - gold are
f
ff
f
ff
25
blow - ing;
mf
blow - ing, are blow - ing; But they shall gleam with
mf
mf

28
gleam a - gain, gleam a - gain,
f
spi - ri - tual glint - er, gleam, gleam a - gain, gleam a -
gleam, gleam a - gain, gleam,
f
gleam a - - gain,
f
31
gleam a - gain, gleam a - gain, gleam a - gain.
mf
-gain, gleam a - gain, gleam a - gain, gleam a -
gleam a - gain, gleam a - gain, gleam a -
mf
gleam a - gain, gleam a -
mf
34
mp
-gain.
-gain.
-gain.
mp
mp

37
UPPER VOICES
mp
They shall
SOPRANOS p dolce
S.
mp
S.
A. mp
When pa - ler beau - ty on your brows falls snow - ing, And
T. B.
p dolce
mp

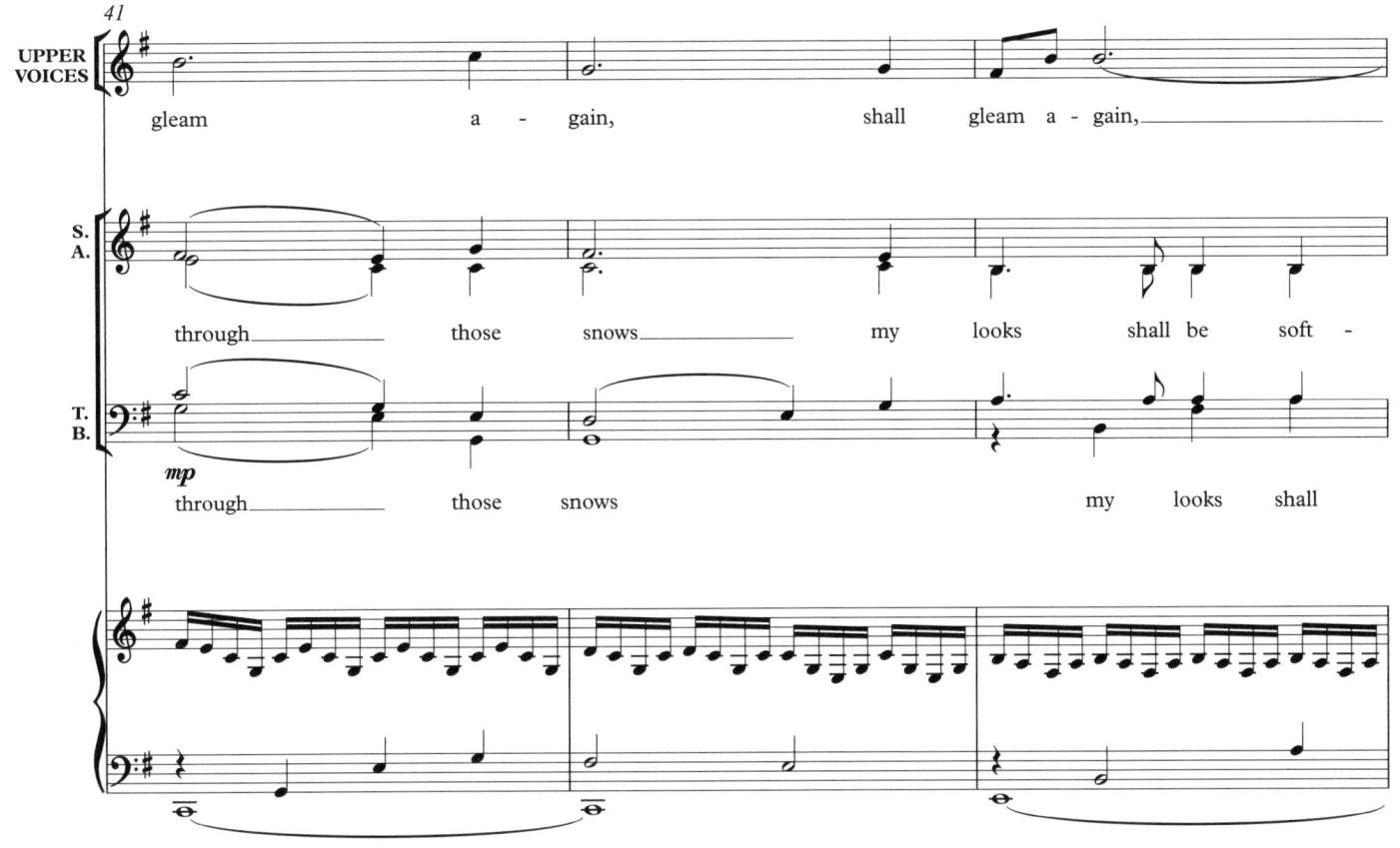
41
UPPER VOICES
gleam a - gain, shall gleam a - gain,
S. A.
through those snows my looks shall be soft -
T. B.
mp
through those snows my looks shall

44
mf
they shall gleam, shall gleam a -
mf
shall be soft -
- go - ing my looks shall be soft -
mf
be soft - - go - ing, soft -
mf
47
- gain.
- go - - ing, soft - go - ing.
p
- go - - - - ing, soft - go - ing.
- go - - ing,
p
3
3
3
3
p

51
mp
mf
The sun, the sun, and
and star - light.
p
mp
mf
The sun may cleanse, And time, and star - light, and
p
mp
mf
mp
mf
57
time, and star - light, and
star - light.
Life will

60
star - light, and star - - -
sing sweet songs, And gods will show us

63
-light. Will sing sweet songs, sweet
plea - sure more than men's.
The

66
songs.
The sum - mer -
The sum - mer - gold shall
The sun - brown and the sum - mer -
sun - brown and the sum - mer - gold are
The sun - brown and the sum - mer -
69
-gold shall gleam a - gain,
gleam a - - gain, they shall
-gold are blow - - - ing, shall
blow - ing, they shall gleam, shall
-gold are blow - ing; shall

72
f
shall gleam a - gain,
gleam a - gain, gleam a -
f
gleam, shall gleam, shall gleam a -
f
gleam, shall gleam a - gain,
f
rit.
Slower
75
mf dim.
shall gleam a - gain.
- gain,
mf dim.
- gain, shall gleam a - gain.
mf dim.
they shall gleam a - gain.
rit.
Slower
mf dim.
p
pp
Ped.

SNARE DRUM

2. *Spring Offensive*

BOB CHILCOTT

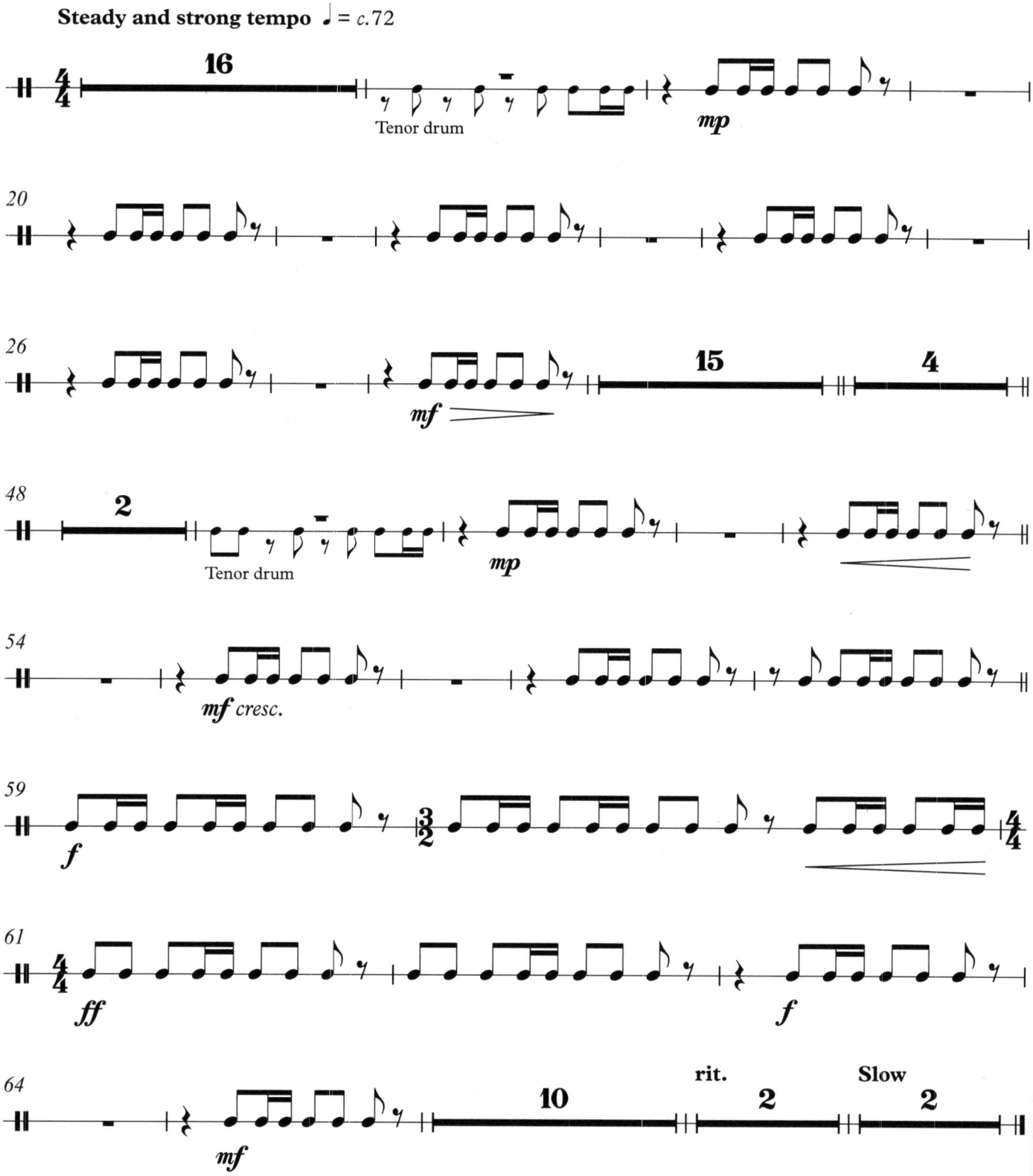

© Oxford University Press 2018. Photocopying this copyright material is ILLEGAL.

TENOR DRUM

2. Spring Offensive

BOB CHILCOTT

© Oxford University Press 2018. Photocopying this copyright material is ILLEGAL.

SOLO CELLO

3. *Apologia pro Poemate Meo*

BOB CHILCOTT

© Oxford University Press 2018. Photocopying this copyright material is ILLEGAL.